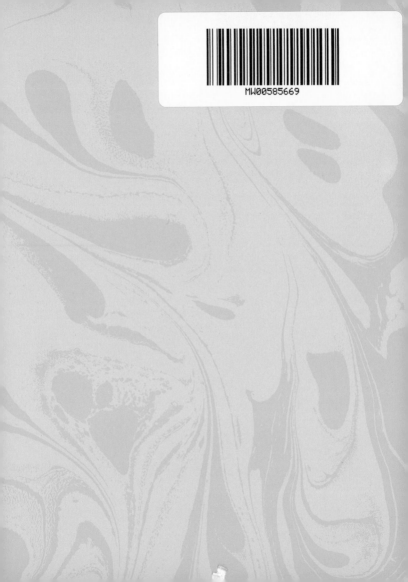

MANIFESTING

LIVE *your* DREAM LIFE

✦ ◆ ✦

GAIA ELLIOT

Hardie Grant

BOOKS

PART I

✦

PART II

✦

THE MANIFESTS

Manifesting...

PART

· I ·

Introduction

The world often feels a mysterious and challenging place, but it is also one in which we develop our strengths, ideas and talents. We may sometimes feel uneasy about the way ahead and unsure of how we can manifest our dreams, hopes and ambitions. At times like these we need to look to the innate wisdom of the universe and learn to work with and trust it.

In 2006 the idea that you could manifest positive outcomes in your life gained greater awareness when Rhonda Byrne published her exploration of the subject in *The Secret*. She had been influenced by an earlier book, *The Secret of Getting Rich* by Wallace Wattles, published in 1910. The notion of the universe's secret is also embodied in the biblical quote from Matthew 21:22: 'And all things, whatsoever ye shall ask in prayer, believing, ye shall receive.' The idea of manifesting a positive outcome has existed for millennia.

The meaning of manifestation is 'to make things happen' – and so often we feel that we just can't do this, we don't know how, and that this possibility lies outside our control. But this is not true. Sometimes taking control is as simple as just saying 'No' – a powerful word which many of us find difficult to use. More often, taking control means making considered and thoughtful decisions, working with what resources you already have and what is within your capacity to access – and building on this.

6

There is a metaphorical magic in doing this work, and this book will show you how to harness it. With a positive mental attitude we can focus more clearly, and intentionally align our energy more specifically to our aims. We can then manifest outcomes that support our hopes and dreams.

Whatever your life's path, you have more power than you realise and the answers you seek are closer than you think. Believing this is the first step; realising it through the mindful use of manifesting is the second – and this book will help you to do that.

The universe and its power is a resource available to you through the natural world, your relationship with yourself and with others, and your overall attitude to life. When this approach to life becomes a way of being, then you know you are more than capable of manifesting opportunities and attracting what you want.

While this sounds very simple – as if we can change our lives with a snap of our fingers – the truth lies in authenticity: we get better results when what we want aligns with our higher purpose, when it is right for us. It's not always possible to see immediately what our higher purpose might be, but it stems from a belief that to achieve your dreams you need to access your best intentions. While positivity is important, banishing all negative thoughts is impossible. Negative thoughts can also serve as useful challenges: through processing them, you are able to focus and overcome mental blocks, enabling you to manifest what it is you want or need in order to make the progress you desire.

TIMING

Time is a construct we impose on our lives, necessary to schedule a meeting or catch a train; but in reality it is not always obvious that something will change in an hour, a day, a week or even a year. Sometimes we have lessons to learn before our intentions manifest, so trust the process and it will become clear in time. Trust that time is your friend.

The bible says: 'To everything there is a season, a time for every purpose under heaven' (Ecclesiastes 3:1), so bear this in mind as it can free your expectations and allow you to focus on the journey as much as the destination.

8

The Law of Vibrations

Every living and non-living thing in the world vibrates at a frequency and these frequencies are a measurable aspect of energy. When we become aware of this – think of how good someone else's positive energy can make you feel – we can begin to learn how to generate and attune to this positive energy and use it to create an aura and field of attraction. Then, within this state, you can use the vibrational energy of intention to attract to you what you need and manifest new possibilities.

The physical impact of endorphins – those feel-good chemicals in our bodies – can also affect our energy levels, and how we think and feel. These chemicals can be accessed to lift and focus our mood through exercise or thinking differently about something. Clearing old energy patterns by reducing ruminating thoughts can be encouraged by physical exercise; while walking through beautiful scenery can lift your mood as much as a good night's sleep.

9

We know how exhilarating it is when our mood is high – we feel supercharged and capable of anything. Conversely, we all know how hard it is to function when we are unwell or our mood is low – we are easily distracted and unfocused.

Our energy levels constantly fluctuate and are a combination of our physical and psychological state. Mind and body interact and regulate how we feel, and there is nothing woo-woo about this! Do you ever get irritable when you haven't eaten? Does laughing with a friend make you feel good? Someone's energy levels can also affect yours: happy engagement with someone you care about can give you a lift, while someone's sadness or despair can bring you down. Our connectivity with the world around us can raise or lower our energy.

Understanding that our own thinking can change our behaviour is the basis of cognitive behaviour therapy (CBT). Anyone can change unhelpful thought patterns to their advantage. It's more than just positive thinking. By challenging old thought patterns you can prevent them from inadvertently sabotaging your best efforts to make the changes you seek. Be aware of what effect these unhelpful thought patterns might have on your energy and seek to address them.

The Law of Attraction

If you want to manifest positive change in your life, you need to understand the Law of Attraction. The principle of like-attracts-like works by putting out positive energy into the world and having the expectation that it will be returned to you in equal measure. A quick test of this is smiling at someone: it's almost impossible not to smile back. We are built for positive connection and when this occurs, it enriches and energises us all.

Always punch up, not down. Even if you feel negatively about someone or a situation you can't change, don't let it make you feel powerless because you can always change how you feel about it. This in turn empowers you and gives you agency and authenticity. Saying 'No' to something that feels unhelpful, or putting yourself first in a situation, doesn't come easily to many people, but doing so can often help reveal the next steps to manifesting your aims, and in turn this can avoid resentment build-up which blocks energy.

11

The Power of Intention

Aligned with the Law of Attraction is the Power of Intention. Setting your intention can really help focus your mind. Not only that, but it can also help you focus on what you might need to do to realise your intention – otherwise it's like setting out on a journey without having a sense of where you want to go.

Manifesting what you want doesn't happen through chance or fate. It happens because you make it so, and understanding this helps you to see that by energising your thoughts through intention, you are supporting the actual manifestation of your hopes and desires.

12

Five Steps to Manifest Change

Remember, you cannot change others, but you *can* change the way you think and feel about them and this can be very powerful. This may include doing things differently or not doing anything at all. The choice always rests with you, and you will know what choice is best aligned to your higher purpose. The five steps don't always happen in the sequence they are set out in this book, but are always a feature of manifestation.

1. ASK

You are entitled to ask for what you want but you may not always receive *exactly* what you want. If you are clear about your expectations you will receive what you *need*. Asking for something specific enables you to focus your energies and manifests greater possibilities for its outcome.

2. BELIEVE

Believing that you are allowed good things can sometimes take practice, especially if you have low expectations in life. Belief also arises from the tangible evidence that when you put your hopes and dreams into words, when you focus on and articulate these (see Step 1), you have a better chance of creating the energy to manifest them. Reframing old beliefs that you may still be clinging to can help you let go of inhibiting energies.

3. TRUST

Trust is a key component of manifesting. It comes partly from the self-belief that you can rely on attracting good energy by putting it out there. But remember that the timing of things might be dependent on elements outside your control – so do what you can to facilitate good timing, then trust that the universe has your best interests at heart.

4. LET GO

Once you have focused your intention, let go of the need to control every aspect of it, which is the equivalent of constantly pulling up a plant to see how its roots are growing. This is quite difficult for many of us: we internalise the belief that only by holding something in mind, focusing on it to the exclusion of all else, will it yield results.

5. RECEIVE

Sometimes we find it difficult to receive good things and find it hard to believe we are worthy. If your expectations are low, the negatives in life can feel like a self-fulfilling prophecy, as you fail to receive the good things that are available to you. And practise gratitude, so that you may recognise again and again what's good in your life and the positive energy this creates.

15

A NOTE ON
POTENTIAL BLOCKS

One of the biggest blocks to manifesting is resistance. Here, the idea of positive change or beneficial outcomes feels scary and we resist the idea of it.

That's when your internal critic is your own worst enemy – that voice that says, 'You don't deserve it, and if you ask for too much you will be denied it.' A lifetime of low expectations can be hard to overcome. Start small, challenge those negative assumptions and sit with how that makes you feel. Be open to the idea of change as a positive energy. Then allow yourself to accept the notion that improving your life lies within *your* power.

Sometimes what's within your control is just as simple as smiling at your neighbour, exchanging pleasantries with a shopkeeper, or paying a friend a compliment. These small actions create the possibility of positive energy. And what you give out will return to you. You are *paying it forward* and utilising the Laws of Attraction, attracting positive vibes that help make things happen.

16

Tools for Manifesting

There are several aspects of manifestation
that are useful to know about and use, and these
are referred to as tools. Understanding the role of
each will help you feel your way into manifesting
outcomes you want. Use these tools until
manifesting becomes an attitude,
a frame of mind, a way of life.

17

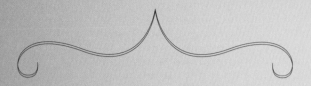

VISUALISATION

If you are a visual person you may always see things in your mind's eye – both good or bad – mapped out ahead of you, and visualisation may come easy to you. For others, it may take some practice.

Visualising what's good in life and what you want to manifest is key because it helps you see it is actually possible, rather than having a vague, abstract idea of it. It can also help you see what might be needed to get you to a particular point – what you might need in terms of help or input – and this can be really useful.

18

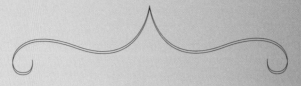

RITUAL

There are reasons why people like rituals – whether it's an individual or regular group practice like yoga, a rite of passage like a wedding or a funeral, or simply the making and sharing of a pot of tea. Rituals foster a sense of connectivity with ourselves, with other people in our social or work community, with the natural world and the universe. They help us to feel connected and that connectivity fosters a sense of inclusion, purpose and self-motivation that can help bolster confidence and productivity.

When it comes to manifesting your hopes, dreams and desires, you may find that an element of ritual – and this can be something personal you do at home, like creating a mood board – will help you articulate and focus on your intention, conveying this to the universe and bringing energy to the possibilities that will open up to you.

19

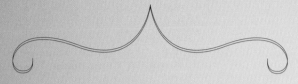

SETTING INTENTIONS

When it comes to manifesting, setting a clear intention is extremely valuable because it pinpoints what you want. You can then visualise it and call into existence the outcome you want. You are also able to recognise how it aligns to your higher purpose.

Setting an intention can also help you see what you need to do to accomplish it, which helps when it comes to manifesting the outcome you want.

Take your time when setting an intention for a particular outcome: imagine, visualise, make notes, reflect, clarify and consider, so that you have a complete sense of what it is you want to manifest, rather than a half-baked idea. That way your energetic intention is clear and can find reflection in the universe and wider world.

INTUITION

Intuition is what some call a 'gut instinct' but generally that instinct is built on accumulated experience – so what feels automatic and intuitive is often a learnt skill, although at an unconscious level. Why do I mention this? Because many people find it difficult to trust their intuition. Sometimes, if their gut instinct might take them out of their immediate comfort zone, they will ignore or override it – in doing this, they can miss a useful intuitive nudge in manifesting their hopes and dreams.

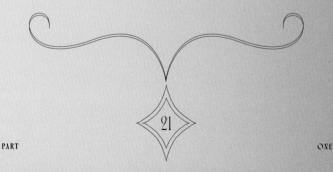

21

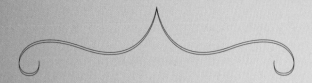

AFFIRMATIONS

Affirmations are positive statements that can reinforce your intentions. An aspect of positive thinking, affirmations don't deny that life can often feel tricky, but they encourage you to look to what is good in life – and build on it.

Affirmations encourage you to think differently or more creatively about what you want. Focusing on a positive affirmation also allows you to reframe any negative thoughts that can transpire against our best efforts to manifest the outcomes we want and deserve.

22

You have the tools, the universe is absolutely on your side, and now you can open your heart to all sorts of possibilities by manifesting what you want from life – in your relationships, your work and your creativity. It's all available to you.

Part 2 the book, on the following pages, is broken down into seven categories, with five suggestions for manifesting in each, designed to help you focus and set your intentions. You may begin to recognise manifestation themes that run through each category – and as you shift your general mindset to one that is open to the possibility of manifesting what you want, you will find that you can more easily recognise what works for you in terms of ritual, visualisation or affirmation.

Soon, manifesting will be your go-to attitude – and, in time, you will find the universe opening up to you in an affirmative way. Trust the process, trust the universe and trust yourself!

23

PART

The
Manifests

◆ II ◆

Manifesting
Friendship

Friendship is the starting point of many relationships, but can often feel troublesome to realise. Friendships are important – they allow us to explore and discover aspects of ourselves, our capacity for human interaction and for love. Remember to put your own values first and look for similar values and interests in others on which to build your friendships.

· 1 ·

Actively seek the joy in life and run with it.

What might it look like
to spend time with a friend?
Talking, walking together, enjoying
a meal? Visualise this and the form
of a friendship you wish to manifest
will become more recognisable to you.

· 2 ·

How you choose
to show up determines
what will show up
for you.

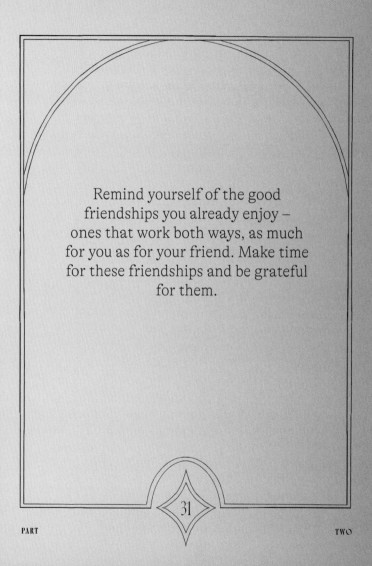

Remind yourself of the good
friendships you already enjoy –
ones that work both ways, as much
for you as for your friend. Make time
for these friendships and be grateful
for them.

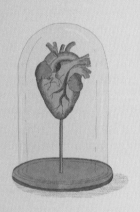

3

If it doesn't enhance your life, it doesn't belong in your life.

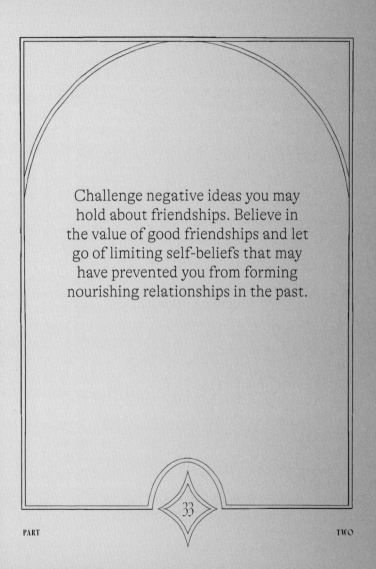

Challenge negative ideas you may hold about friendships. Believe in the value of good friendships and let go of limiting self-beliefs that may have prevented you from forming nourishing relationships in the past.

33

Don't hang on to
those things that no
longer serve your
higher purpose.

Respect your boundaries – and theirs.
Being immediately too full-on and
over-intimate can be off-putting.
Friendship is an interplay of your
needs and wants as much as theirs.

Ask yourself if
what you are doing
now is getting you
what you want.

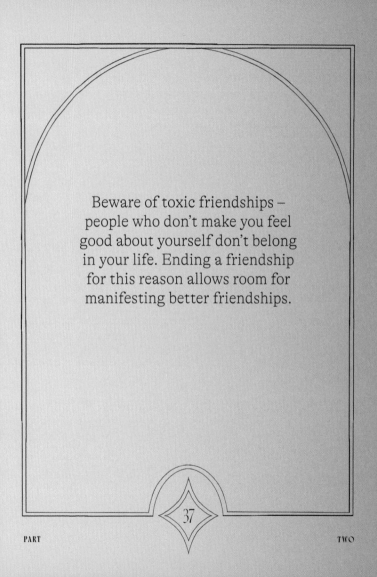

Beware of toxic friendships –
people who don't make you feel
good about yourself don't belong
in your life. Ending a friendship
for this reason allows room for
manifesting better friendships.

Manifesting Love

The human heart is built for love and the universe thrives on it, but sometimes it can seem hard to find. Look first to yourself and the beliefs you hold about love in your life. Remember that love is not finite – the more you love, the more love you have to give. But guard against giving it away to those who don't value the gift you offer them.

Let your hopes
not your hurts shape
your future love.

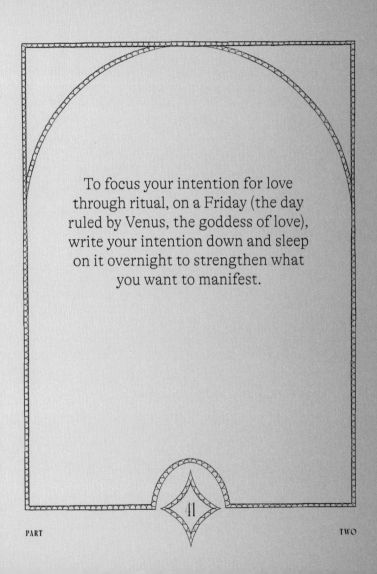

To focus your intention for love
through ritual, on a Friday (the day
ruled by Venus, the goddess of love),
write your intention down and sleep
on it overnight to strengthen what
you want to manifest.

41

· 2 ·

Be open to alternative
thoughts and ideas.

Make a mood board to help you
visualise the role of intimate love
in your life. You may not yet know
the person you seek, but you can start
to anticipate how they might make
you feel – and this will help you
manifest love.

43

· 3 ·

A
compassionate
heart starts
with oneself.

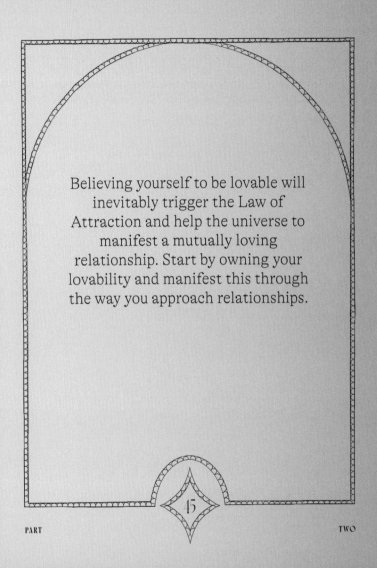

Believing yourself to be lovable will inevitably trigger the Law of Attraction and help the universe to manifest a mutually loving relationship. Start by owning your lovability and manifest this through the way you approach relationships.

· 4 ·

Let go of everything you are not, and cherish what you are.

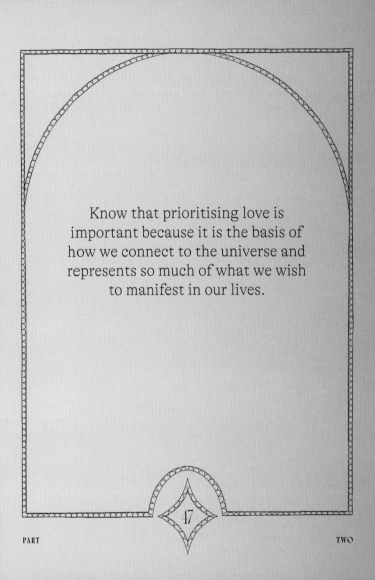

Know that prioritising love is important because it is the basis of how we connect to the universe and represents so much of what we wish to manifest in our lives.

It takes courage to
risk love, but it is
always worth it.

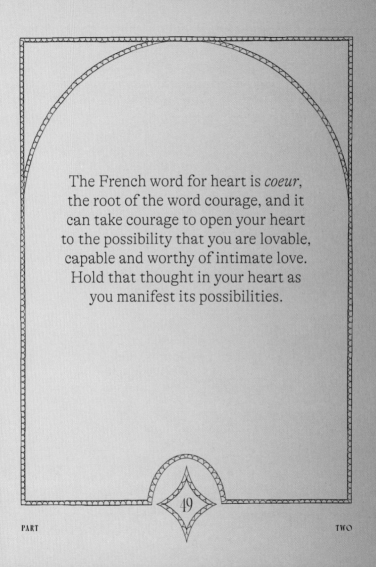

The French word for heart is *coeur*,
the root of the word courage, and it
can take courage to open your heart
to the possibility that you are lovable,
capable and worthy of intimate love.
Hold that thought in your heart as
you manifest its possibilities.

Manifesting Better Health

Our physical and mental health are
very much aligned with our energies –
when these are in harmony, we function
better in the universe. Ensure you place
value on your health and take care of it.

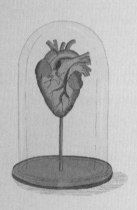

Adversity can be
a wake-up call –
listen to its message.

If you find yourself consistently functioning below par, then your physical body is telling you something. Manifest better health through some basic self-care – improved diet, more exercise, prioritise sleep – and the universe will take care of the rest.

· 2 ·

All human wisdom can
be distilled into one
statement: live in hope.

Living in shame or defeat
is the antithesis of what the
universe offers – and those
self-limiting beliefs will prevent
you from living your best life.
Practise gratitude for what you
have, to reignite what hopes
you can manifest.

Something special waits
for you every day –
your job is to find it.

If you don't look out for what's good in life, and express gratitude for it, you may miss out on what the universe is offering you. When it comes to manifesting better physical and mental health, adjust your mindset first.

You don't need to
see the whole staircase
to take the first step.

The first step in any self-help regime is setting your intention. Your intention doesn't need to include an outcome or time frame, but you do need a clear intention to actually begin. Once you set your intention, the steps needed to manifest its possibilities will become clear to you.

5

Grow strong roots to ground you against adversity.

The capacity to recover from physical
or mental ill-health requires resilience
and a continual commitment to invest
in yourself, and prioritise what will
ensure that you bounce back.
Manifesting this is the result
of that investment.

Manifesting a New Job

Perhaps you enjoy your job but feel the
need to extend and challenge yourself,
or maybe you hate your job and need to
leave. Either way, the time is right for
a new position, role or even career.
Take from the experience and expertise
you have already gained to maximise
and manifest the next step.

· 1 ·

Optimism and
hard work make the
world go round.

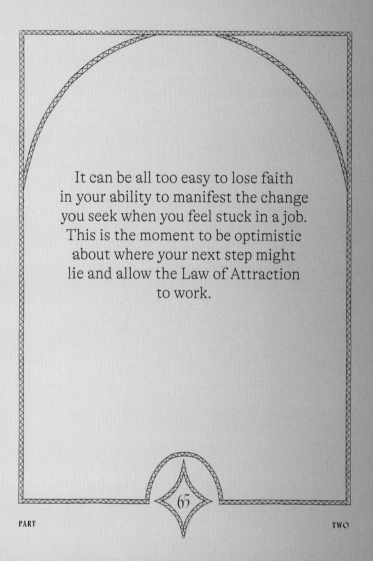

It can be all too easy to lose faith
in your ability to manifest the change
you seek when you feel stuck in a job.
This is the moment to be optimistic
about where your next step might
lie and allow the Law of Attraction
to work.

65

If you don't join this
game called life, you
can't expect to win.

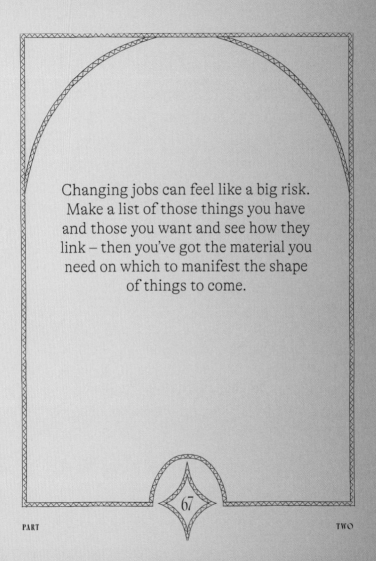

Changing jobs can feel like a big risk. Make a list of those things you have and those you want and see how they link – then you've got the material you need on which to manifest the shape of things to come.

· 3 ·

Information
is the fuel
to motivation –
find out what you
need to know.

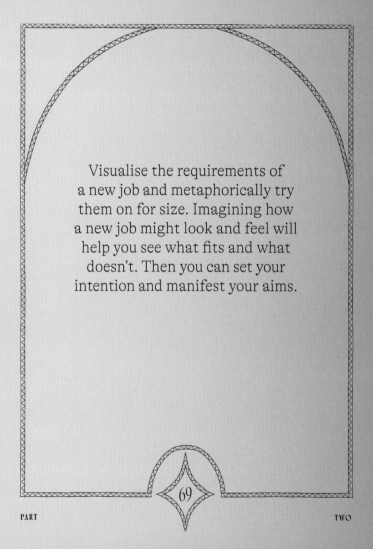

Visualise the requirements of
a new job and metaphorically try
them on for size. Imagining how
a new job might look and feel will
help you see what fits and what
doesn't. Then you can set your
intention and manifest your aims.

69

· 4 ·

Strive always for
progress not
impossible perfection.

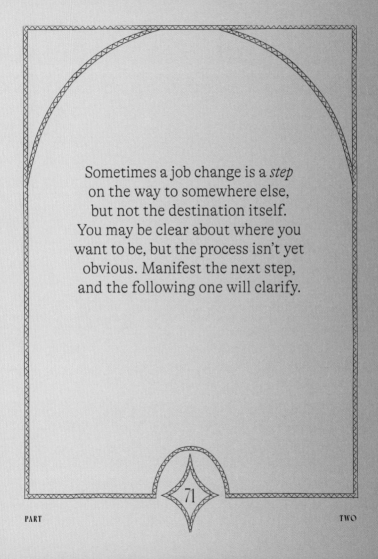

Sometimes a job change is a *step*
on the way to somewhere else,
but not the destination itself.
You may be clear about where you
want to be, but the process isn't yet
obvious. Manifest the next step,
and the following one will clarify.

71

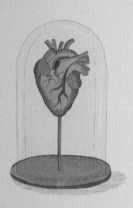

Be patient when
you have nothing
and grateful when
you have everything.

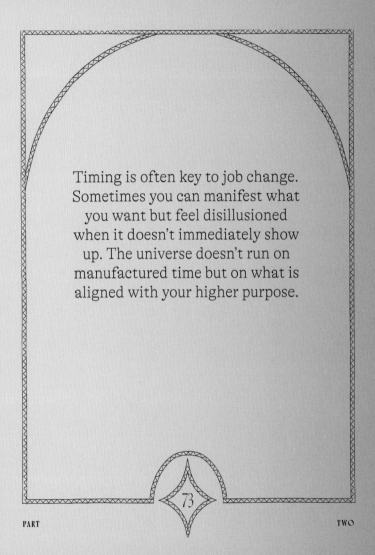

Timing is often key to job change. Sometimes you can manifest what you want but feel disillusioned when it doesn't immediately show up. The universe doesn't run on manufactured time but on what is aligned with your higher purpose.

73

Manifesting
Change

For some, the very idea of change and
moving out of our comfort zone is scary.
Turn that fear into excitement about
the opportunities that will emerge
when you embrace and manifest the
positives that change can bring.

1

Mistakes offer
us a wonderful
opportunity,
a learning curve.

How often have you felt that a mistake is a disaster, when in fact it's just something you did that wasn't successful? Learn from mistakes and use these insights to manifest the change you would like to make in the future.

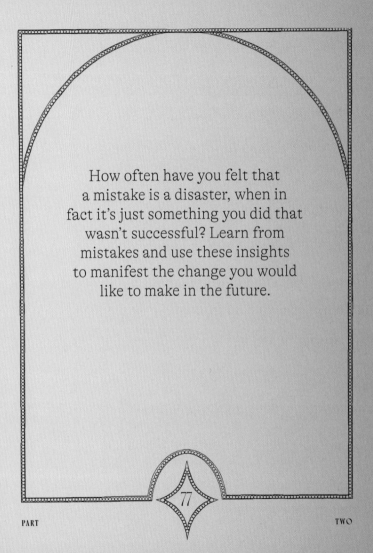

77

2

Do not let your past
define you, but prepare
you for the way ahead.

No one has a perfect life, but that need not prevent you from improving yours. Create a mood board of what you would like more of, and this will help you manifest the changes you need to make it happen.

· 3 ·

Distinguish between the
things you can and
can't change, and
prioritise the former.

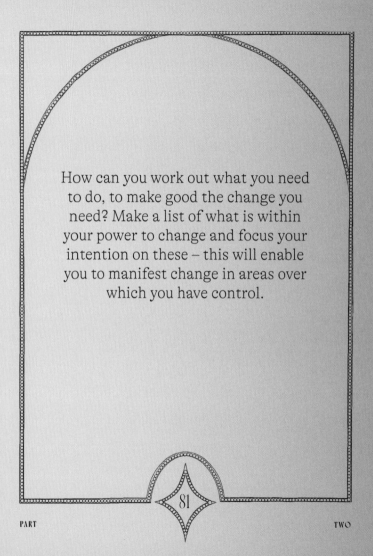

How can you work out what you need to do, to make good the change you need? Make a list of what is within your power to change and focus your intention on these – this will enable you to manifest change in areas over which you have control.

The only true
constant
in life is change –
embrace it and
its possibilities.

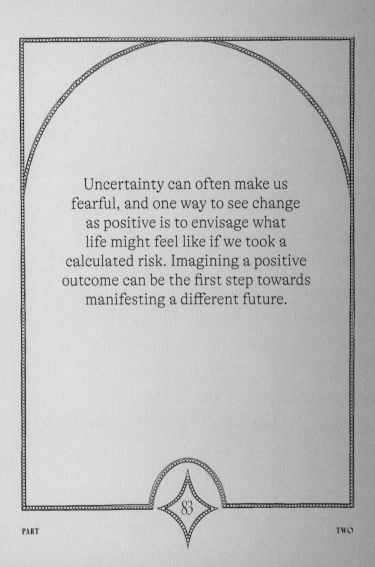

Uncertainty can often make us
fearful, and one way to see change
as positive is to envisage what
life might feel like if we took a
calculated risk. Imagining a positive
outcome can be the first step towards
manifesting a different future.

· 5 ·

Identify the positive
changes you want, and
notice when you've
made them.

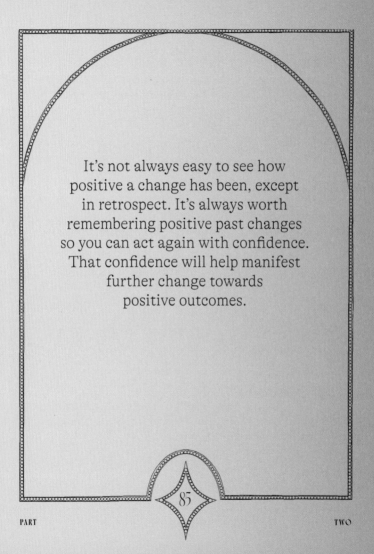

It's not always easy to see how positive a change has been, except in retrospect. It's always worth remembering positive past changes so you can act again with confidence. That confidence will help manifest further change towards positive outcomes.

85

Manifesting Abundance

Abundance very often starts from a place of gratitude. Acknowledging the bounty of what the universe offers each and every one of us is a first step towards making that abundance more meaningful and sharing it more widely. This acknowledgement also helps to challenge any self-limiting beliefs that could inhibit abundance in our personal good fortune.

Believing in yourself is a quality that is attractive to others.

Create a mood board with pictures, doodles and words that signify abundance to you. Consider what abundance looks like when it comes from your work, social and love life. Where do you need to focus?

· 2 ·

Celebrate your efforts
as well as your
achievements.

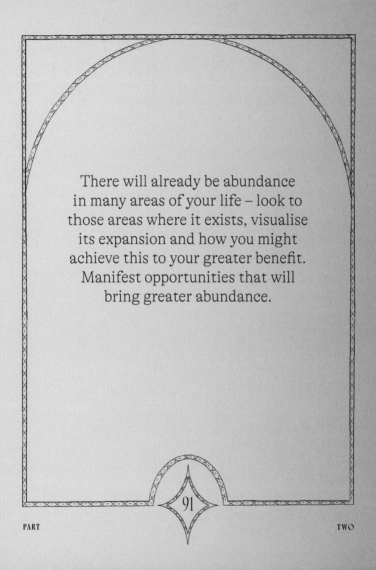

There will already be abundance
in many areas of your life – look to
those areas where it exists, visualise
its expansion and how you might
achieve this to your greater benefit.
Manifest opportunities that will
bring greater abundance.

91

· 3 ·

Simplifying your
life improves the mental
clarity with which
you can focus
on your goals.

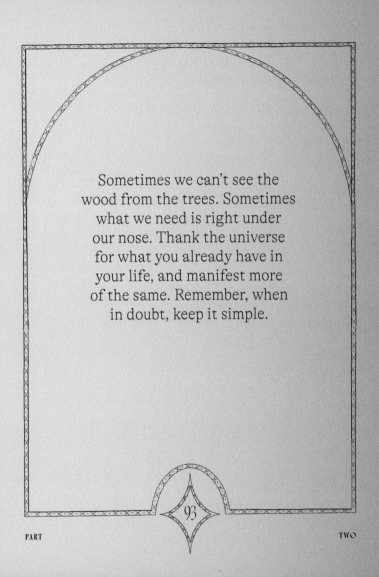

Sometimes we can't see the wood from the trees. Sometimes what we need is right under our nose. Thank the universe for what you already have in your life, and manifest more of the same. Remember, when in doubt, keep it simple.

93

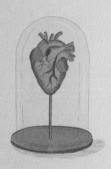

4

Ignore what could
go wrong and focus
on what is going right.

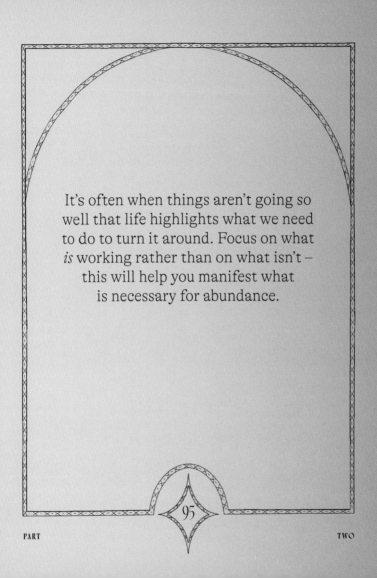

It's often when things aren't going so
well that life highlights what we need
to do to turn it around. Focus on what
is working rather than on what isn't –
this will help you manifest what
is necessary for abundance.

95

· 5 ·

It can take a
dark night to make
visible all the stars.

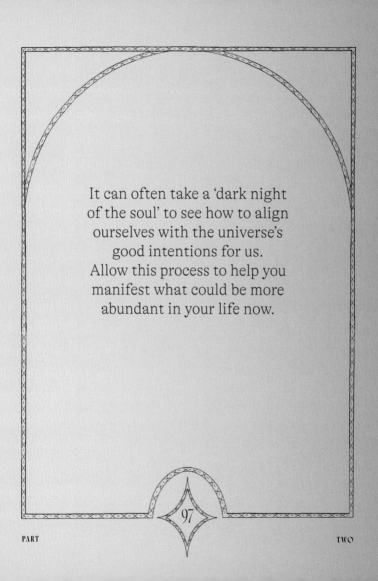

It can often take a 'dark night
of the soul' to see how to align
ourselves with the universe's
good intentions for us.
Allow this process to help you
manifest what could be more
abundant in your life now.

97

Manifesting the Home You Want

Home is where the heart is, and where we start from. It's where we should feel secure and completely ourselves. If this isn't currently where you find yourself, then it's time to manifest the home you want – not just the bricks and mortar, but the space it offers in which you can flourish and grow.

1

The choices you
make tell people
who you are.

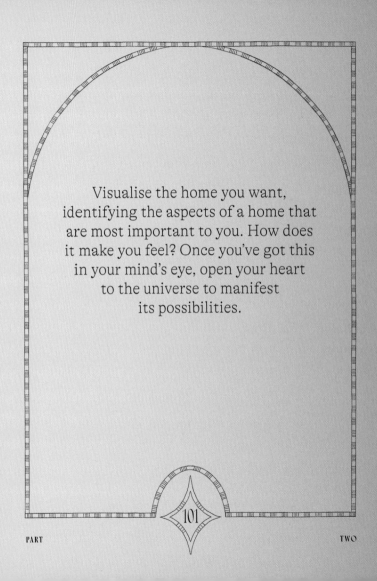

Visualise the home you want,
identifying the aspects of a home that
are most important to you. How does
it make you feel? Once you've got this
in your mind's eye, open your heart
to the universe to manifest
its possibilities.

101

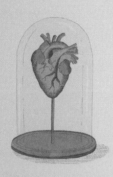

2

Don't linger too long anywhere that hurts your heart.

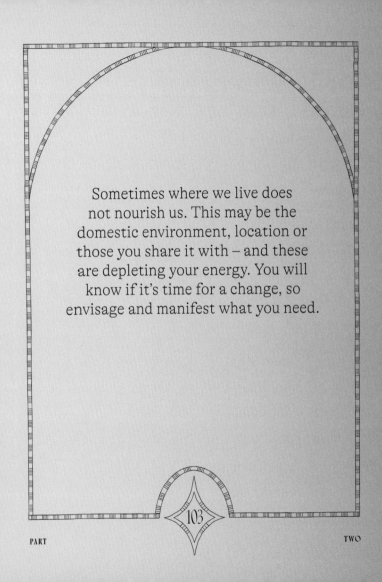

Sometimes where we live does not nourish us. This may be the domestic environment, location or those you share it with – and these are depleting your energy. You will know if it's time for a change, so envisage and manifest what you need.

· 3 ·

If your current plan
isn't working, change it
– but always stick to
your goal.

What we call home and what
we need from it can change, but
it should always nurture our energy.
Clarify your intention in alignment
with what you now need, and
manifest the possibilities for that.

· 4 ·

Everything you are
going through now is
preparing you for
what comes next.

You may feel very clear about what home means and can recreate it over and over again. Or you may still be searching. Trust the universe that all lessons learnt will help you to finally manifest what you want and need.

5

If the door doesn't
open, it's not for you
- look for another
one that does.

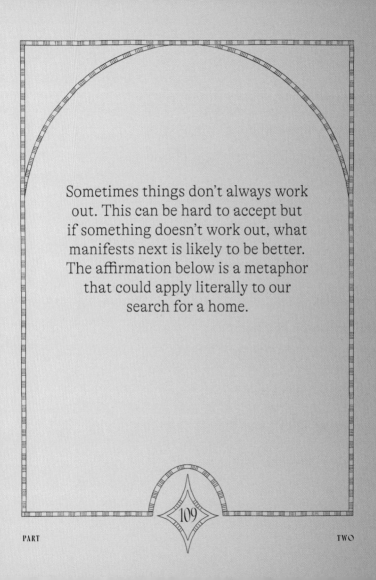

Sometimes things don't always work out. This can be hard to accept but if something doesn't work out, what manifests next is likely to be better. The affirmation below is a metaphor that could apply literally to our search for a home.

Acknowledgements

First and foremost, thanks are due to
my inspirational and creative publisher
Kate Pollard, who is always willing to
go the extra mile to produce books of
substance and beauty. My thanks also to
illustrator, Lucy Pollard, and the design
team at Evi-O.Studio for creating such
a gorgeous series of books. Thanks are
also due to my teachers – past and
present – who inspire me on my journey
as an esoteric practitioner, enabling me
to develop my own skills and talents.
And to my Romany grandmother who
provided insights and access to a world
beyond our immediate reality.

Finally, to my family on this journey
we call life, thank you for your support
and love.

About the Author

Gaia Elliot is a green witch based in London. She loves tending to her garden and being surrounded by the abundance of nature, which feeds into her spell-casting and magic-making. Gaia believes that anyone can harness their inner power by tapping into their intuition. She has a strong interest in Tarot, the power of the moon and psychology. Gaia's spiritual journey started when she was a young woman, and she loves nothing more than helping other people to start or continue their own. She is author of *The Book of Answers* and *Pocket Mystic: Emergency Spells*, also published by Hardie Grant.

Published in 2024 by Hardie Grant Books (London)

Hardie Grant Books (London)
5th & 6th Floors
52–54 Southwark Street
London SE1 1UN
hardiegrantbooks.com

British Library Cataloguing-in-Publication Data.
A catalogue record for this book is available from
the British Library.

Pocket Mystic: Manifesting
ISBN: 978-1-78488-965-4
10 9 8 7 6 5 4 3 2 1

Publishing Director: Kate Pollard
Copy Editor: Hannah Boursnell
Proofreader: Gill Hutchison
Design and Art Direction: Evi-O.Studio
Illustrator: Lucy Pollard
Production Controller: Martina Georgieva
Colour reproduction by p2d

Printed in China by
RR Donnelley Asia Printing Solution Limited

MIX
Paper | Supporting
responsible forestry
FSC® C018179
www.fsc.org